Christmas at Home

101 SIMPLE HOLIDAY CRAFT IDEAS

WRITTEN AND COMPILED BY
ELLYN SANNA

BARBOUR
PUBLISHING, INC.
Uhrichsville, Ohio

Published by Barbour Publishing, Inc., P.O. Box 719, Uhrichsville, Ohio 44683
http://www.barbourbooks.com

 Member of the
Evangelical Christian
Publishers Association

Printed in Canada

Table of Contents

Somehow the things we make ourselves always seem closest to our hearts. Maybe that's because we are made in the image of a Creator God who delights in creativity. At any rate, Christmas is a wonderful time for making pretty things, and the crafts included in this book will give your own creativity plenty of inspiration. Use these crafts as gifts; use them to make your home more festive; use them as a chance to enjoy time together with your children—but whatever you do, use them to celebrate the birth of our Savior!

1

Crafts for Kids

At Christmas and always,
Lord, I thank You for the children in my life.
May these simple crafts help them learn
to give the best gift of all:
their hearts.

Candy-Filled Cookie Cutters

A colorful addition to the family Christmas tree!

MATERIALS:

pencil
open-style cookie cutter of desired shape
lightweight cardboard
scissors
clear tape
nuts or small candies in holiday colors
corsage bag (available in floral shops)
8 inches of ribbon

Place the cookie cutter on the cardboard and trace, then cut out shape. Tape the cardboard to the back of the cookie cutter. Fill with brightly colored candies or cookies of your choice. Put the treat on a flat surface and slide corsage bag around the cookie cutter; tie open end with a ribbon.

Gingerbread People

Another child-made ornament to add charm to your tree!

MATERIALS:

pencil
gingerbread man
  cookie cutter
scissors
medium-grade sandpaper
cinnamon stick
measuring spoons

powdered white tempera
  paint
white glue
bowl
squeeze bottle
hole punch
yarn

Using a gingerbread man cookie cutter as a pattern, trace and cut out shape on the back of the sandpaper. For gingerbread smell, rub the sandy side of sandpaper with the cinnamon stick. In a bowl, stir together two teaspoons of paint with four tablespoons of glue; spoon into squeeze bottle. Draw features and details of gingerbread man with squeeze bottle, let dry, and hang by a yarn threaded through a hole punched in top of gingerbread man.

Snow Globe

As a child, remember how fascinated you were with snow globes? Children will be delighted to make their own with this easy recipe!

MATERIALS:

baby food jar and lid
felt
2 tsp plaster of Paris
1 tsp water

tiny plastic figures
decorative accessories
1/2 tsp tapioca

Mix water and plaster of Paris to form a thick paste. Place a small mound on the inside of the lid, and press figure (Santa, reindeer, snowman, etc.) and decorations in plaster in a standing position just before it sets. Allow plaster to harden and fill jar with clean water. Sift tapioca through medium strainer and then finer strainer to remove powder; add to jar of water to serve as snow. Cover lid top with felt and screw on tightly. Invert and shake!

Message Minders

Here's a good gift for Grandma!

MATERIALS:

clothespins

newspaper

clear plastic spray enamel

enamel paint and brush, paint pens, or
  permanent fine-tip markers

tiny stickers

magnetic tape
  (self-adhesive)

Lay out clothespins on several sheets of newspaper. Lightly spray with clear plastic enamel and allow to dry. Decorate with stickers, or paint with designs of your choice; let dry. Cut a length of magnetic tape for back of clothespin.

Starchy String Ornaments

*Hang these from a light fixture or chandelier,
in front of windows, or on the tree.*

MATERIALS:

thick cotton string   colored cellophane
liquid starch   white glue

Place string in liquid starch to soak. Arrange in desired shapes on
top of colored cellophane and using white glue, drizzle all around
each shape; lay another sheet of cellophane on top and allow to
dry. Cut out around the outside of the string shapes; punch holes
through tops and string.

Bookmarks

Makes a great gift for an aunt or uncle!

MATERIALS:

pencil	felt	ribbon
scissors	white glue	paint pen

Create your own patterns in the shape of flowers, tennis rackets and balls, footballs, baseballs, or other small objects. Draw around each pattern 2 times on felt and cut out. Create your own detailing with paint pen, or make details with contrasting pieces of felt and glue. Select a coordinating piece of ribbon and glue matching pieces of felt to both ends in order to make back and front identical, and let dry.

Paper Snowflakes

These make pretty package decorations, as well as ornaments.

MATERIALS:

aluminum foil, gift wrap,
   tissue paper, or
   construction paper

manicure scissors
yarn

Cut paper into circles. Fold in half, then again in thirds, fourths, or more. Trim around the top to square or round off, and cut notches of different shapes into the sides. When opened you have your own unique snowflake design.

Hot Cocoa—Instant Mix

*Put this mix in the Gift Bag craft that follows and
you have a holiday gift for neighbors or teachers.*

INGREDIENTS:

2 cups nondairy creamer
1½ cups sugar
½ cup unsweetened cocoa

½ cup nonfat dry milk
½ tsp salt

SERVING DIRECTIONS: Add boiling water to 2 to 3 heaping teaspoons, stir and serve.

Gift Bags for Cocoa Mix

To create your fun gift bag:

Choose an animal (a reindeer, for instance) that you'd like to make from a small, colored sack. Draw and cut out the mouth and cover the hole with plastic wrap. Use stickers for eyes and nose, or cut out and paste on your own. For antlers, trace around your handprints with bright magic markers; cut out and glue to bag. Put Cocoa Mix inside, then fold top of sack back, tape edges, and attach a tag with serving directions.

Candy Cane Reindeer

*Hang this from your tree—
or pass out a bunch to friends at school!*

MATERIALS:

candy canes
2 white chenille stems
  (pipe cleaners)
scissors
white glue

2 plastic wiggly eyes
red pom-pom
thin green ribbon
jingle bell
fishing line

18

Twist one chenille stem around the curve in the candy cane for antlers. Cut the other stem in half and twist one around each end of the first stem, turning up ends to create antler look. Glue pom-pom to bottom of curved end for "Rudolph nose" and wiggly eyes above. Pull ribbon through the opening at top of jingle bell and tie around "neck" of reindeer for bow. Attach a loop of fishing line.

Angel Ornaments

Each completed angel will be as unique as a child's handprint.

MATERIALS:

white poster paint
stiff blue paper
markers
white glue

glitter glue
clear contact paper
gold cord

Have children dip their hands in white poster paint and transfer handprints to blue paper in a fan pattern. Let dry and cut out to create angel wings. Cut out an angel head (circular shape) and body (triangular shape) from additional paper and glue wings and head to body. Children may draw details of faces, hair, and angel gowns. Add glitter to a sparkly halo. Place completed angel between 2 sheets of clear contact paper and cut around outer edge to laminate. Punch a hole in the top and hang with gold cord.

Basket of Christmas Eggs

Dyeing eggs is so much fun—
why not do it at Christmas as well as Easter?

MATERIALS:

wax crayons or melted paraffin wax   egg dye
hard-boiled eggs   ribbon
green plastic berry basket   Spanish moss

Paint Christmas designs on hard-boiled eggs with crayons or paraffin and dip into egg dyes. Use holiday-colored ribbons to decorate berry basket and fill with Spanish moss to display eggs.

Frosty Flakes

*This frosty, spiky ornament will delight
small craftspeople—and bigger ones too!*

MATERIALS:

newspaper	ornament hanger
round toothpicks	white acrylic paint
white glue	paintbrush
1-inch plastic foam ball	can of spray snow

Spread out newspapers to protect work area. Dip one end of each toothpick in white glue and stick in plastic foam ball until ball is evenly covered with toothpicks. Push an ornament hanger into top of the foam ball. Paint the toothpicks and ball with white paint and allow to dry. Spray snowflake with spray snow, dry, and spray again.

Tub-Time Toys

*This is a fun gift for an older sibling to make
and give to a baby brother or sister!*

MATERIALS:

pencil
paper
scissors

felt-tip marker with
permanent ink
soft sponges (variety of colors)

Create your own animal patterns (duck, fish, alligators) and cut
out. Draw around each pattern on a dry sponge using the felt-tip
marker. Soak the sponges in water and then squeeze them out as
dry as you can. Cut inside the marker line with scissors, squeezing as you cut.

Pom-Pom Wreaths

These can be used as either ornaments or presents.

MATERIALS:

white glue
package of green pom-poms
package of tiny red pom-poms

wooden drapery ring
narrow ribbon
red embroidery floss
(or string)

Glue green pom-poms one by one onto drapery ring until completely covered and ring looks like a wreath. Glue a few tiny red pom-poms onto wreath for berries. Let dry. Pull a festive patterned ribbon through the hook on the ring and tie. Hang from embroidery floss pulled through the hook.

Decoupage Band-Aid Boxes and Candy Tins

Little girls won't be able to resist these pretty containers for trinkets and treasures.

MATERIALS:

acrylic paints in colors of your choice
small paintbrush
flowers cut from cards, gift wrap, or wallpaper
glue
can of spray varnish
wide band of lace (for bottom of candy tin)

Paint tins inside and out. Cut out flowers to fill surfaces and glue all over front, top, and sides. Coat with spray varnish. To create an elegant effect on candy tin, a wide band of lace may be glued around bottom portion instead of flowers.

Heavenly Mints

*Younger children will need help with the cooking,
but they'll enjoy turning these sweets into
angelic Christmas favors or tiny presents.*

INGREDIENTS:

1 (16 ounce) package powdered sugar
½ cup margarine, softened
2 tbsp evaporated milk
4 to 5 drops of peppermint flavoring
2 to 3 drops of food coloring

Mix ingredients in a large bowl at high speed until well blended. Knead mixture until smooth. Spread paper towels over cookie sheets. Shape mixture in rubber candy molds and place shapes on cookie sheets; cover with paper towels. Mints should stand overnight and then be stored in covered containers with waxed paper between layers.

Wrap each mint in plastic wrap. Then create your own angel pattern and draw angels on stiff colored paper; cut out. Punch 2 holes in the center of each angel and pull a thin ribbon through each hole. Tie ribbon around a wrapped mint to attach it to the angel.

Egg Carton Christmas Choir

This slightly goofy choir will make your kids laugh!

MATERIALS:

egg carton
scraps of felt or yarn in yellow,
   brown, orange, tan, and white
fine-tip markers

uncooked
   elbow macaroni
scrap paper
craft glue

Cut yarn or felt scraps into pieces about $\frac{1}{8}$-inch x $\frac{3}{8}$-inch. After turning egg carton upside down, apply glue to top of each "bump" to which "hair" (yarn or felt) may be glued. You may want to work on one bump at a time so that glue doesn't dry between choir members. Make details of each face with fine-tip markers. Pierce 2 tiny holes at the bottom front of each choir member and insert macaroni pieces curving inward for hands. Glue tiny pieces of sheet music (folded in half and decorated with notes) between macaroni hands.

Customized Stamp-Printing

*Your kids will enjoy creating
custom-made Christmas cards, poetry, and artwork.*

Stamps may be carved or cut into shapes from:

sponges
corks
fruits/vegetables
gum erasers
pasta shapes

rope or string formed
    into desired shape
cookie cutters
textured household items

Use a pre-inked stamp pad purchased from an office supply or stationer's store, and stamp on the following suggested surfaces:

white or brown craft paper
construction paper
tissue paper
paper bags
cotton
muslin

linen
shelving paper
stationery or note cards
rice paper
any absorbent fabrics

Colored Ice Candles

Children will need adult help with this craft—
but it makes a beautiful gift for
teachers, grandparents, or almost anyone!

MATERIALS:

empty (quart-size) milk carton
candle wicking
pencil
scissors
cracked ice

3 bars of paraffin wax
empty coffee can
cooking pan
crayon
old wooden spoon

Completely open the top of the milk carton. Tie one end of candle wicking around the middle of the pencil. Measure string the length of the milk carton, placing pencil even with the top of the milk carton; cut. Rest the pencil across the top of the milk carton, allowing wick to hang down the middle. Fill carton with cracked ice and place in the freezer. Fill a cooking pan half full of water and turn heat to "very low" (should be done with adult supervision). Place three bars of paraffin wax in the empty coffee can and put coffee can in pan of heating water. When wax has melted, turn off the stove. Removing paper from colored crayons, break desired colors into paraffin one at a time and stir with a wooden spoon until desired color is achieved. Remove milk carton from freezer and have an adult pour the melted wax over the ice in the milk carton, filling almost to the top. As the ice melts, pour off the water. Set carton aside until wax hardens. Placing carton in sink, remove sides of carton, untie wick, and trim.

Clay Townspeople Candlesticks

*These one-of-a kind creations will become part of
your family's treasured Christmas collection—
a decoration young artists will greet each year with pride and delight.*

MATERIALS:

newspaper
package of self-hardening clay
bowl of water
small sponge

modeling tools
  (toothpicks, pencil, spoon)
garlic press
candle

Spread newspapers over work area. Take first piece of clay and roll into a coil 10 inches to 11 inches long. Pinch ends together to make a circle. Roll several more coils, each one smaller than the last, stacking circles until a body is formed. Dampen fingers or sponge with water and smooth edges of the coils together to hide seams. Roll a small ball of clay for the head and smooth line between head and body. Roll another coil and cut in half for arms. Add arms to body and blend, creating shoulders. Add clay buttons or belts, and using a toothpick or pencil, poke holes for eyes and mouth. Create hair by squeezing clay through garlic press. Add fabric bows, scarves, hair ribbons, or something for your creation to hold, such as tiny wrapped presents, etc. Roll a coil to place on top of head to hold the candle. Place in a sunny spot and dry for several days.

Caramel Corn in a Gift Bag

Remember this sweet holiday tradition from your childhood?
Now you can reexperience the fun with your own children.
And you'll end up with a great gift for the neighbors!

INGREDIENTS:

1 cup butter or margarine
½ cup light corn syrup
2 cups brown sugar
1 tsp salt

½ tsp baking soda
1 tsp vanilla
5 quarts popped corn

Preheat oven to 250 degrees. In a large saucepan, melt butter over low heat. Add brown sugar, corn syrup, salt, and stir. Turn heat to high and bring to a boil for 5 minutes, stirring constantly. Remove from heat and stir in soda and vanilla. Distribute popcorn evenly between 3 13-inch x 9-inch pans. Pour cooked mixture over popped corn and stir. Bake for 1 hour, removing from oven every 15 minutes to stir, to ensure even coating. Pour caramel corn onto countertop that has been covered with wax paper and cool. Break into pieces.

Give caramel popcorn in small, personally designed boxes to which colorful drawings, cutouts, and pieces of Christmas wrapping have been glued. Line box with colored tissue paper and fill with caramel corn.

More Simple
Christmas Ornaments
for Kids to Make:

• Tie ribbon or yarn around top petals of a pinecone for hanging, and glue beads on cone as ornaments.

• Using red and white pipe cleaners, twist together and form into a candy cane shape.

• Cut various shapes (reindeer, angels, Christmas trees, Santa) out of various colors of felt (in duplicate). Glue a Popsicle stick to bottom piece of felt; then glue top piece over all. Decorate with sequins, cord, glitter, beads, etc. Punch a hole and tie on cord for hanging.

Encourage Christmas Creativity in Little Ones with the Following Activities:

- Provide old white gloves on which finger puppets may be painted, or socks and paper bags that can be turned into puppets.
- Pour liquid starch into jars and add food coloring to make homemade finger paint.
- Use old greeting cards to create a Christmas collage place mat (cover with clear contact paper to laminate), or glue them to cardboard backings and cut jigsaw-style to make puzzles.
- Make your own cutout dolls and cutout gift wrap for clothing.
- Use construction paper, milk cartons, crayons, and glue to make a Christmas village.

2

Christmas Tree Ornaments

O Christmas tree, O Christmas tree,
How lovely are your branches.

*Lord, may our Christmas tree's evergreen be a symbol
to us of the unending life we have in Jesus.*

Sparkling Prisms

Add some sparkle to your tree!

MATERIALS:

chandelier prism (available at home center stores)
wire ornament hanger
12-inch piece of ribbon

Simply attach an ornament hanger to the top of the prism and
tie a dainty bow (something Victorian and lacey looks nice) at
the top, allowing the ribbon ends to trail down the sides of the
prism. This technique can also be used to create unique ornaments using old pieces of cast-off jewelry.

Golden Lamé Ornaments

These shiny ornaments are quick and easy.

MATERIALS:

½ yard gold lamé
½ yard white polyester backing
cotton and metallic threads
small bag of polyester stuffing

Draw simple star and crescent moon patterns on paper, about 3 inches across. Fold fabric in half with right sides together; pin on patterns and trace outlines with a pencil. Cut through both layers adding a $1/4$-inch seam allowance. Baste along penciled outline leaving a $1\frac{1}{2}$-inch hole for stuffing. Machine stitch using $1/4$-inch seams and clip seams at angles of star arms and at $1/4$-inch intervals on concave curve of moon. Turn shapes right side out and fill with polyester filling. Hand-stitch opening closed and run metallic thread through tip of each ornament for hanging.

Cinnamon Ornaments

These spicy-scented decorations add a homespun flavor to your tree.

INGREDIENTS FOR CINNAMON DOUGH MIX:

½ cup white glue   1 cup boiling water
1¼ cup ground cinnamon

MATERIALS:

plastic bag   small knife   rolling pin
cardboard   emery board   wax paper

Mix glue and boiling water in a bowl; stir in 1 cup cinnamon and mix well. Knead dough for 4–5 minutes; seal in plastic bag and let sit for 1–2 hours. Trace a simple pattern for head and trunk of angel (1 piece about 5 inches long) on cardboard and cut out. Roll out dough on wax paper that has been sprinkled with cinnamon to a thickness of ³⁄₈ of an inch. Using pattern, cut out angel shapes with small knife and pierce holes in trunk with a pencil for ties where legs and arms will attach. Allow cutouts to dry 2–3 days on a clean, dry surface dusted with cinnamon. Turn daily. Some shrinkage will occur. Use emery board to smooth any rough edges after drying. In the event cutout cracks, mix 1 tablespoon of cinnamon and 1 teaspoon of glue with boiling water to make thin paste and fill in cracks.

MATERIALS FOR ANGEL ORNAMENT:

completed cutout—from page 47
4 cinnamon sticks
¼ yard of jute
1 yard of brown cord
20 tiny cedar pinecones
24 dried cranberries
4 whole cloves
6 large bay leaves
hot glue gun and glue sticks

To make legs and arms, loop length of cord through each hole on cutout and through 1 cinnamon stick; glue end of each limb securely. Make 4 small jute knots to glue to end of each appendage and trim excess. Glue tiny pinecones along bottom front of cutout as skirt; use cloves for buttons and adouble row of cranberries for hair. Fan bay leaves out behind angel head and shoulders and glue to back of cutout. Glue loop of brown cord at back for hanger.

Nature's Ornaments

Place orange rings cut in ¼-inch slices on an oven rack at lowest temperature and dry for 1 hour. Just below the peel, push a hole through with knife tip and thread with a ribbon and tie to tree.

Bundle together 3 or 4 cinnamon sticks with a pretty ribbon and glue cranberries to the ribbon with a glue gun; place bundle on tree branches.

Thread tiny kumquats onto medium stub wires and loop circlets over tree branches or tie with contrasting ribbons.

Jeweled Christmas Balls

*The Christmas lights will make
these decorations glitter and shine!*

MATERIALS:

solid-colored round
   Christmas ornament
juice glass
tweezers

round multicolored jewels
   (available in craft stores)
tacky glue
gold glitter paint pen

Set ornament on juice glass to stabilize; using tweezers, dip jewels in tacky glue and arrange on upper half of ball; allow to dry. Using paint pen, circle each jewel and dry. Turn ornament over and repeat for bottom half.

Terra-Cotta Pot Bells

*For those who enjoy a little
Southwest flavor in their decorating.*

MATERIALS:

2-inch terra-cotta pot
artist's gesso
acrylic paint
brushes

red metallic pipe cleaners
jingle bells
glue gun

Paint patterns with southwestern themes (such as cactus, chili peppers, geometric shapes, etc.) onto the bell with gesso. When completely dry, paint over with bright colors of acrylic paint. Thread 1 pipe cleaner up through bottom of pot and form a loop for top of "bell." Form 3 pipe cleaners in a bundle and attach to the top of the pot with the first pipe cleaner. Then wrap the pipe cleaner around the bundle and thread back through hole in the pot. Attach jingle bells to the ends of the pipe cleaner with hot glue.

Fruits and Treasures Garland

A unique garland to add beauty and life to your tree.

MATERIALS:

tan pearl cotton
large-eyed needle
dried limes, oranges,
   artichokes, corn kernels
cinnamon sticks
assorted nuts
bay leaves

small pinecones
small wooden cutouts:
   hearts, block, disks
miniature baskets
miniature bird nests
wooden beads
drill with $\frac{1}{16}$-inch drill bit

Cut pearl cotton to a length of 50 inches. Thread end through needle. Pierce assortment of above materials with a needle. If any of the objects are too difficult to pierce, drill $1/16$-inch holes with drill bit. String each item onto pearl cotton with needle, pulling each back snugly to make room. Knot ends of pearl cotton when garland is complete.

Etched Glass Ornaments

These lovely ornaments are easier to make than they look.

MATERIALS:

clear round glass ornament
white vinegar
¼-inch-wide masking tape
paint pen (available in craft, discount, and fabric stores)
star stickers
rubber gloves
etching cream (available in art, craft, and discount stores)
paintbrush
key chain
sprig of greenery

Before starting, clean glass ornament with hot water and white vinegar. (Be sure not to reintroduce finger prints to areas which will be etched.) Use paint pen to draw snowflake designs and/or masking tape to create stripes. Press star stickers firmly to ornament. After paint has dried, put on rubber gloves and etch ornament according to instructions using brush and etching cream. Wash off etching cream, and carefully remove stickers, tape, and paint. A beautiful frosted or etched surface will remain. Thread key chain through ornament hanger and tuck spring of greenery into top of ornament.

Lace-Embossed Clay Tree Ornaments

Lovely to give away—and just as lovely to keep!

MATERIALS:

modeling compound clay
luncheon-size plate
masking tape
pieces of old lace or paper doilies

talcum powder
1- x 8-inch dowel rod
small straw
gold or silver thread

On a protected work surface, tape luncheon plate face down and lightly dust with talcum powder. Roll a 1-inch ball of modeling clay to an even thickness in the center of the plate using the dowel rod. Place lace or doily over the clay and roll again to emboss pattern into the clay. Remove lace and push straw through top of the ornament to form a hole through which metallic thread may be strung to hang ornament. These ornaments may also be painted the color of your choice if desired.

Beaded Snowflakes

*Make a bunch of these—
and give them out to members of your
Sunday school class or prayer group.*

MATERIALS:

corsage pins with pearl ends (available in craft and fabric stores)
crystal-like beads in desired shapes
small cork
iridescent white glitter paint pen (usually used for fabric,
    available in craft and discount stores)
monofilament thread

Make 2 sets of 4 beaded corsage pins, and 1 set of 2 beaded corsage pins, for a total of 10 beaded pins. Make each set distinct from the other by placing the beads on the pins in a specific, prearranged pattern. Leave last ¼ inch without beads on each pin. Cut the cork if necessary, so it is about ¼ inch long. With the round side of the cork laying on the work surface, poke 1 beaded pin into the cork (close to work surface) like the spoke of a wheel. Place a matching beaded pin opposite the first. Place the remaining 2 opposite each other, between the first set. Using the remaining set of 4, poke each into the cork, slightly closer to the top of the cork and alternating with the first set of 4. Place the remaining 2 beaded pins into each round end of the cork. Paint cork using glitter paint pen. Dry and apply a second coat if necessary. Cut a desired length of monofilament and tie to 1 spoke of snowflake to hang.

Heart-Sachet Tree Ornaments

A homespun ornament to keep or give.

MATERIALS:

fabric
pinking shears
thread

potpourri
ribbon

Cut 2 pieces of fabric (cut through 2 layers at once) with pinking shears in the shape of a heart. With wrong sides of fabric together, machine-stitch around heart close to pinked edge, spooning in a tablespoon of potpourri when half sewn. Finish sewing and attach a ribbon loop to hang from tree.

3

Holiday Decorations for Your Home

You are the Guest we welcome, Lord.
May our homes reflect the joy in our hearts at Your birth.

Pomanders

*Pomanders were first made in the Middle Ages to
scent rooms and sweeten the air,
and to give fragrance to linens and clothes.
They make lovely additions to arrangements and gift baskets.*

MATERIALS:

citrus fruits (oranges, lemons, clementines, kumquats, and limes)
whole cloves
1/2-inch-wide tape, to mask pattern
nail or darning needle
orrisroot powder
1/2-inch-wide ribbon

The traditional pattern for a divided orange is made by wrapping tape around the fruit in crisscrossing directions to divide it into 4 equal segments, but you can make a geometric pattern of your choice, or stud the fruit all over with cloves. Use a nail or darning needle to pierce the skin of the fruit in the pattern you have designated and push cloves in each hole. When the design is completed, put the fruit in a paper bag and sprinkle 1 tablespoon of orrisroot powder for each large fruit and close the bag. Leave for 2-3 weeks, allowing the fruit to dry and the spices to mellow. Remove the masking tape and decorate with ribbons.

Metal-Foil Ornaments

These make striking ornaments to hang in front of a window.

MATERIALS:

metal foil, in brass, copper, and aluminum
    (available from craft or specialist metal suppliers)
ballpoint pen
metallic thread (for hanging)

Draw a shape onto stiff paper and cut it out to create a pattern. Put the pattern on a piece of metal foil that is slightly larger than the pattern, and draw around it using a soft pencil. Place the foil on a pile of magazines with the pattern on top in the same position; remove ink cartridge from a ballpoint pen and go over the outline with the empty pen, pressing very firmly. Remove the pattern and use the pen to draw freehand within the outline to create details, remembering to press hard all the time. Use a pair of strong scissors to cut out the design and pierce a hole at the top. Tie a loop of metallic thread through for hanging. Flatten foil gently with rolling pin if it has curled. The right side is the opposite side to the one worked on, which gives the metal a raised, "embossed" effect.

Victorian Tableau

Add a touch of Victorian nostalgia to your home.

MATERIALS:

12- x 18-inch unpainted shadow box frame
   (available at craft stores)
gold spray paint
14- x 20-inch piece of fabric in a solid color
   (silk moiré works well)
glass to cover the tableau
masking tape
glue gun
cardboard ornaments
pictures cut from magazines or cards

Christmas craft novelties
silk or dried flowers and greenery
photocopied sheet music
cup of brewed coffee

Spray frame completely with gold paint after removing back. Cover the frame backing with solid fabric, gluing or taping on back side. Photocopy a sheet of Christmas music. To create an aged look, place sheet music on a cookie sheet and spritz with water. Pour a cup of coffee evenly over the paper and bake in a 200 degrees oven for a parchment effect. Roll sheet music diagonally around a pencil to curl and place it in the center of fabric-covered board. Arrange craft novelties, cardboard ornaments, silk flowers, and greenery to fill in bare spots. When pleased with your design, hot glue in position one at a time. Place glass in frame, refasten back, and attach a wire to hang.

Candy Wreath

...ament away for next year—or eat it this year!

MATERIALS:

wire coat hanger
green and red curling ribbon
2½ pounds hard candy wrapped at both ends
3-inch-wide green or red velvet bow

Bend the hook of the coat hanger into a loop for hanging, and shape the bottom of the hanger into a circular form for the wreath. Cut ribbon into 12-inch pieces, one for each piece of candy. Curl the ribbon and tie each candy onto the hanger until the entire hanger is covered with candy. Tie bow to the top of the wreath.

Mitten Doorknob

These can also be used to hold a small present or gift certificate.

MATERIALS:

purchased mitten (pretty knit with holiday patterns and colors)
scissors   medium-weight wire
tissue paper   wire cutters
greenery   fabric bow
cinnamon sticks

To give mitten shape, stuff with tissue paper and add cinnamon sticks and greens to spill from the top. Attach a wire hanger to opposite sides of the mitten top for hanging over doorknob, and tie a fabric bow to one side of hanger.

Ribbon Tree

...... holiday color to your table with this centerpiece.

MATERIALS:

5-inch styrofoam ball
12-inch wooden dowel or squared wood trim, for stem
basket
ready-to-mix cement
selection of ribbons in different colors and widths,
   about 6½ yards of each
florist's spool wire
reindeer moss

Spear the Styrofoam ball on the dowel. Mix enough cement to almost fill the lined basket and pour in. Place dowel in center of basket and secure with a web of masking tape across the top of pot. Let dry for 24 hours. Cut ribbon in strips 7 inches long. Double up ribbon to form single-loop bows and twist wire around center, leaving 1 long end to stud ball completely with bows. Spread reindeer moss out over base of tree.

Gilded Pinecone Arrangement

*This centerpiece will add a touch of
nature's bounty to your home.*

MATERIALS:

pinecones

nuts

cinnamon sticks

chestnuts

large and small pomegranates

bay leaves

nutmegs

gold metallic enamel paint

old cake rack

large container such as
   an old urn or bowl

golden gauze ribbon

Dip the above and allow to drip-dry on rack placed over paint
bucket (about 20 minutes). Arrange in chosen container and tie
gold ribbon around bottom.

74

Gingerbread-Friends Garland

This garland will give your home a "country" feel.

MATERIALS:

clay gingerbread men
red and white icing

⅛-inch-wide red ribbon
scissors

Using oven-bake clay, make a batch of gingerbread men. Punch holes in each hand with a drinking straw and bake. After the "cookies" have cooled, outline and decorate using icing. Link the men together by threading thin ribbon through holes in their hands. Knot ribbon and trim the ends. Drape over mantel or along edges of country cupboard.

Winter Wonderland Centerpiece

*Remember the old song
"Walking in a Winter Wonderland"?
Now you can bring the scene inside!*

MATERIALS:

white styrofoam, 3 feet x 2 inches x 8 inches long
double-sided tape
white birch branches, 12 to 18 inches long
white Christmas lights with white cords and
  battery pack if possible
spray fixative
iridescent snow confetti

Place double-sided tape on bottom of Styrofoam so that it is secured to table. Stick branches into Styrofoam to achieve a forest effect. With lights lit, distribute them evenly among branches. Spray branches with fixative and sprinkle snow confetti over them, as well as Styrofoam base.

Crystallized Fruit Bowl

These fruits are as beautiful as they are delicious!

MATERIALS:

assorted fruits: lady apples, pears, grape clusters,
   plums, nectarines, cherries, lemons

egg white   aluminum foil

superfine granulated sugar   bowl for display

Spread sugar over a large plate. Using a pair of tongs, dip each piece of fruit into egg white and shake off excess; roll gently in sugar until completely coated. Place on aluminum foil to dry and arrange in a favorite bowl.

Doorknob Jingle Bell

*This quick and easy decoration will ring out
the sounds of the season every time you open your door.*

MATERIALS:

lightweight wire   wire cutters
red berry cluster   sprigs of evergreen
large gold jingle bell (available at craft and fabric stores)
1¼ yards of 2-inch-wide sheer ribbon

Wire berry cluster and evergreen together; run wire through hanging loop of jingle bell. Thread ribbon through hanging loop and tie a bow in ribbon about 7 inches above the ornament.

Marbleized Centerpiece

An easy and fun way to make an elegant centerpiece!

MATERIALS:

clear glass Christmas ornament with removable top
squeeze bottles of liquid acrylic paint in colors of your choice
   (available at craft and discount stores)

Squeeze about 1 teaspoon of paint into ornament from which top has been removed. Add the second color of paint in about the same amount. Turn the ornament repeatedly, swirling the paint inside to create the marbleized effect. Replace ornament top when dry and put ornaments in a clear bowl with coordinating beaded garland.

4

Christmas
Sewing Crafts

*May the work of my hands enrich Your kingdom, Lord.
May I spread Your love with each thing I make.*

Grandma's
Little Christmas Stockings

*Cute to use as decorations, package toppers,
or to hold tiny gifts or a rolled up bill.*

MATERIALS
(to make seven stockings):

1⅛ yards off-white cotton or muslin;
  matching thread
assorted tan and off-white tatted lace and crochet scraps
assorted off-white buttons
assorted tan buttons
assorted tiny brown shells

Create a simple stocking pattern approximately 3 inches wide x 12 inches long and cut out 14 stocking shapes. Sew stocking fronts to stocking backs with right sides facing. (All seam allowances are ¼ inch.) Leave top edges open. Turn under ¾ inch and slipstitch. Cut scraps of tatted lace 4 inches long to use as hangers for each of the 7 stockings. Tack to top edge of heel seams. Clip stocking curves and turn right side out. Decorate with lace, buttons, crochet scraps, and shells. May also be spruced up with holly or mistletoe.

Ribbon Pillow

Makes a beautiful gift!

MATERIALS:

assortment of antique ribbons, each 13 inches long
2 13-inch squares of solid color fabric
stuffing for 12-inch pillow
pushpins
board
cording

Attach square of fabric to board with pushpins. At upper left corner of fabric, place one ribbon going horizontally and another vertically. Using traditional basket weave, add ribbons along the top and side, weaving in and out until square is completed. Pin ribbons to the fabric and then remove from board. Sew ribbons down and attach second piece of fabric as backing. Sew on color-coordinated cording all the way around, leaving an opening. Add pillow and stitch closed.

Exercise Pad

For the fitness enthusiast!

MATERIALS:

3 terry bath towels, 26 x 46 inches
1-inch-thick foam pad, 24 x 65 inches (density value of 3 to 3.5)
nylon, self-gripping fabric fastener tape

Cut 1 towel in half crosswise. Remove binding on 1 end of each of the whole towels remaining to stitch together for ties. Sew the raw middle of each half towel to the raw end of 1 of the other 2 towels. With right sides together, pin the lengthwise edges of the towels so they'll fit over the foam. Remove foam and stitch side seams. Stitch strips of fastener tape at both ends, inserting foam to find best position for the tape. Sew the reserved strips of binding together and attach at the center of one end of the cover for use as ties when the pad is rolled up.

Necktie Garland

This garland will add color and charm to any room.

MATERIALS:

a necktie to use as pattern
various fabric scraps
  (Christmas prints)

sewing thread
pearl beads

Make a pattern from the bottom of a necktie (triangular point plus about 2 inches above) and cut shapes from fabrics (2 of each print), adding ¼-inch seams. With right sides facing, sew shapes together in pairs and leave top edge open. Trim the points, turn, and press. Press under top seam and sew closed. Add a pearl to each tip and stitch shapes together at top corners.

Mobiles

Create a variety of mobiles for the little ones in the family using mobile wires (available at craft stores), monofilament thread, and any of the following:

cutout greeting cards
toy airplanes
angels

tree ornaments
tiny stuffed animals

You can also use leftover scraps of fabric to cut out little figures or other Christmas shapes to sew and stuff; anything with bright colors and prints to stimulate baby's eyes. The important thing to remember in composing a mobile is maintaining balance. Begin hanging dangling things from top wires using thread. Adjust lengths of string to balance each side and work downward, adding new wires and hooks to keep in balance. Don't crowd objects together.

Holiday
Dinner Napkins

An inexpensive way to dress up the Christmas dinner table.

Trim a yard of holiday fabric into 17- x 15-inch rectangles and machine hem. Another yard of fabric will make a coordinating table runner.

Lacy Hearts

These make quick and easy party favors.

MATERIALS:

2½-yard piece of 4-inch-wide ruffled lace
candy cane   small silk rose
glue gun   thin piece of ribbon

Sew a casing in lace, starting ½ inch from plain edge. Cut lace in half and insert candy cane into each piece, gathering ruffle as you go. Attach candy canes at bottom and top with glue gun to form a heart. When dry, attach silk rose at center point with glue and affix ribbon loop at back for hanging.

Christmas Laundry Bag

A wonderful December surprise for a college student!

MATERIALS:

1½ yards red burlap background fabric
½ yard contrasting striped fabric (for candy canes)
¼ yard teddy bear panel fabric
½ yard adhesive fabric interfacing
white cording

Place a pillow in the center of the fabric, which has been folded with right sides together. Cut fabric 2 inches wider on sides and 12 inches longer on top end than the pillow. Remove pillow and sew side and bottom seams to create the bag. Machine hem raw edges at top, fold down 6 inches, and press. Pin in place and top stitch; make second row of top stitching $1\frac{1}{2}$ inches up from first row. Separate threads and insert cording for drawstring. Iron contrasting fabric and teddy bear panels to fabric interfacing according to instructions and cut out candy cane shapes and teddy bears. Peel off interfacing, position motifs, and iron.

5

Holiday Candles to Make

You are the Light of the world, Lord.
May my life, too, be a candle that shines
Your love to all around me.

Cookie-Cutter Candles

These candles are as fun and easy to make as they are colorful!

MATERIALS:

sheets of various colored beeswax
  (available at craft stores)
cutting board
cookie cutters

candlewick
  (available at craft stores)
hair dryer

Place sheets of beeswax individually on cutting board. Cut 6 shapes from beeswax using 1 cookie cutter. Insert wick in the center of the wax layers, leaving ½ inch at the top of the candle. Press wax shapes together. If they are not adhering well enough, heat slightly with hair dryer. Be sure to burn candles on a non-flammable surface or on another piece of beeswax.

Candled Apples

A unique gift to show your friendship.

MATERIALS:

13 large yellow apples
13 tea lights or votive candles
lemon juice
footed cake plate

boxwood leaves
lemons or limes
thick toothpicks

To stabilize apples, cut slices from bottoms. Place a tea light on top of each apple, and with a knife trace around candle. Cut down and scoop out enough of apple to allow all of candle to rest below the rim. Sprinkle lemon juice on apple to prevent browning. Cover a cake plate with boxwood leaves and place 5 apples in an evenly spaced circle. Place lemons or limes in center of circle. Stick toothpicks into bottom of 4 of the remaining apples and place on top of lemons, securing with toothpicks. Repeat with 3 more apples and then with last one to create a pyramid.

Frosted Pinecone Candleholders

Use nature's beauty to light up the season.

MATERIALS

12 medium-size,
   upright pinecones
16-ounce box of paraffin wax
2 packages of red wax dye
large, empty coffee can
heavy saucepan

metal tongs
wax paper
wire cutters
12 3-inch to 4-inch
   long red candles
metal spoon

Place pinecones in freezer for 3 hours. Heat water in saucepan over low heat. Place box of paraffin wax in coffee can and set can in saucepan; when wax is completely melted, add wax dye and mix with spoon. Keep heat just warm enough to maintain liquid state. Remove pinecones from freezer and clip out top center of each with wire cutters. Dip pinecones in melted paraffin with tongs, 1 at a time. Drain on wax paper. Holding candle by the wick, dip $\frac{1}{2}$ inch of base into paraffin and stand candle in center of pinecone, pressing downward until candle is securely stuck to pinecone. Drip extra wax around the base of each candle. Cool completely.

Moss-Covered Candle Basket

This makes a one-of-a-kind centerpiece for your holiday table.

Cover a wire basket (without handles) entirely with moss; spray with flame retardant. Nestle candles of various heights and diameters in an assortment of walnuts, pistachios, and other nuts in the shell to stabilize, and light.

Holiday Kitchen Candle

Add some holiday cheer to your kitchen!
This candle makes a fun gift as well.

MATERIALS:

metal kitchen grater
artifical or real holly or any other winter greenery
hot-glue gun and hot-glue sticks
candle
ribbon

Wash grater well and dry. Arrange greenery as desired and glue together. Glue piece to kitchen tool; tie a bow around handle of grater and place candle inside.

Christmas Teacup Candles

*Do you have a special friend you love to meet for tea?
This would be the perfect gift for her.*

MATERIALS:

small china teacup
candle wax
empty coffee can

coloring for wax or old candles
white birthday candles
white glitter

Warm teacups with hot water while wax is melting in coffee can which has been placed in a pan of water on stove. Color wax with candle coloring or old candles; remove from heat. Empty cups and dry thoroughly. Pour wax carefully into cups and allow to set for 2 or 3 minutes or until a soft covering appears on top of wax. Push a birthday candle into the wax and hold until it stands up straight. Add glitter to surface of wax.

Luminarias

For your Christmas gathering or party,
why not use a row of luminarias to
light up the approach to your home?

Punch out designs on small white bakery bags and add sand, gravel, coarse salt, or kitty litter to bottom of bag. Anchor a votive candle placed in a glass holder firmly inside.

Shimmering Centerpieces

Add Christmas luster and beauty to your table.

Group shiny ornaments and metallic, beaded garlands in lovely, shallow dishes (silver or cut glass). In the center, wrap several tapers together with nonflammable festive-colored ribbon or cording. (Be careful not to let candles burn to within 1 inch of ribbon.)

Advent Ring

*Let the humble potato keep
your advent lights safe and stable!*

MATERIALS:

florist's wire
5 small potatoes
circular wire wreath frame
5 white candles
  (or 1 white candle for the center and 4 red ones)

fine spool wire
foliage such as
  holly and boxwood
sphagnum moss

Push a length of florist's wire through each of potatoes; position evenly around ring and attach by twisting wire around the frame. Scoop a hole out of each potato to hold a candle. Cut a slice off bottom of fifth potato to enable it to stand flat and push two lengths of florist's wire all the way through at right angles to each other and parallel to table-top. Scoop a hole out of the center of potato and fix into center of wreath by twisting ends of wires around frame. Bind moss onto wreath frame and cross in middle using spool wire. Pierce potatoes with knitting needle and insert foliage stems (holly, boxwood, and berries) into holes and into moss. Place tall candles in each potato.

6

Wreaths, Swags, and Other Greenery

Lord, as I decorate my home,
I ask that Your Spirit would decorate my heart as well—
trim it with joy, festoon it with peace,
may Your abundant love spill out from me.

Rosebud Wreath

This sweet-scented wreath goes well with a Victorian décor.

MATERIALS:

dampened sheet moss	glue sticks
heart-shaped straw wreath form	dried roses and rosebuds
hot-glue gun	dried bay leaves

Apply dampened sheet moss to straw wreath using hot-glue gun, covering completely. Placing a little hot glue on underside of each flower; press into moss in attractive clusters. Glue dried bay leaves around each cluster of roses. Hang wreath on door or wall, or simply place on a table.

Bright as a Berry

*This "alternative Christmas tree" is
very attractive on a porch,
in front of a fireplace, or in the corner of a room.*

MATERIALS:

glossy evergreen clippings such as boxwood
rose hips
false berries
damp sphagnum moss
1-inch wire mesh netting
wire cutters

7-inch-diameter
  flowerpot
florists' adhesive tape
scissors
florists' scissors

Place the moss on the wire mesh netting and turn corners into center to enclose, crushing into a ball shape. Place ball on the flowerpot and secure with 2 or 3 pieces of adhesive tape. Cut evergreens to approximate equal lengths and push stems in the wire ball until completely filled in. Push in rose hips and false berries.

Ivy Star

Add Christmas elegance to your home.

MATERIALS:

several straight sticks of equal length
glue   terra-cotta pot
raffia   small-leaved ivy plant
wire   fresh moss

Using 6 of the straight sticks, glue together 2 triangles. When dry, lay one over the other to form star shape. Glue together where they intersect and bind with natural raffia. Make a stem for star from 4 to 6 sticks and tie with wire. Attach to stem of star with glue and raffia. Stick stem into pot filled with soil. Plant small-leaved ivy with about 5 long trails and twin around stem and through star. (If a little thin, twine some cut ivy around star.) Cover soil with moss and decorate star with small ornaments.

Kissing Balls

*Don't forget to make this old English tradition
a part of your holiday celebration!*

MATERIALS:

2 wooden embroidery hoops   ribbons, trim, or beads
glue gun   mistletoe
glue sticks

Crisscross wooden embroidery hoops, placing one inside the other, so they are perpendicular, and glue together. Decorate with ribbons, trim, or beads and place sprig of mistletoe in the center. Tie a ribbon at the top for hanging.

Christmas Chandelier

As you decorate your home for Christmas, be creative.
(After all, remember:
We're celebrating the birthday of the Lord of Creation!)

Spray a small twig tree with silver paint, string with strand of clear beads, and stuff with shimmery icicles and hang upside down from the ceiling.

Bay Leaf Wreath

Here's a simple but stunning wreath to make.

Dip bay leaves in gold metallic enamel paint; dry and glue to a twig form in an overlapping pattern until totally covered.

Greenery Clusters

*The evergreen is a symbol of
the eternal life we have in Christ.
What better way to decorate our homes at Christmas!*

MATERIALS:

wire coat hanger	pinecones
12- x 18-inch rectangle of chicken wire	ornaments
greens: cedar, fir, spruce, pine, and holly	ribbon

Pull the coat hanger into a diamond shape and fold chicken wire onto the hanger to create a frame. Tuck greens into the frame working from the bottom up. Cluster pinecones and holly leaves towards top of arrangement and tie a large red bow at top. Hang cluster with hanger hook.

Door Posy

*Add a touch of Christmas to your home that
you'll see each time you go in and out the door.*

MATERIALS

newspaper or scrap paper
fine silver wire
spray paint
scissors
wheat stalks

selection of evergreens such as
    blue spruce, cypress,
    ivy, and yew
dried grasses
2½-inch-wide gold ribbon

Spread newspaper over work surface. Bind together 10 or 12 wheat stalks together with silver wire. Spray wheat and ivy with gold paint and leave to dry. Place evergreens on work surface and arrange other materials over it. Bind stems firmly together with wire and tie ribbon to form a bow. Cut ends slantwise and hang from the door.

Candy Centerpiece

*This wreath for your table will add festive color—
and eating it can become a Christmas tradition!*

MATERIALS:

florists' adhesive clay
  (can be purchased from
  florist's shop)
plastic spike
pedestal cake stand
knife

9-inch-high foam cone
medium floral pins
wire cutters
scissors
dried lavender stems
shiny-wrapped
    hard candies

½-inch-wide ribbon to coordinate with candy wrappers

Press florists' clay onto the base of the spike and place on cake stand. Cut lavender stems in graduated lengths and insert in foam, with longest at bottom extending beyond rim of cake stand, and each successive layer becoming narrower to achieve conical shape. Cut wires in half and push through candy wrappers; twist ends and insert in cone at intervals. Twist a wire around the center of 2 equal lengths of ribbon and pierce ends into top of cone, draping 4 ribbon strips down sides of centerpiece.

Yule Log Candleholder

The Yule log stems from an ancient tradition
that symbolizes the burning of the past as
we celebrate today's new life.

Use a small log, complete with bark and natural imperfections to make a rustic candleholder by drilling holes in the top. Birch, oak, and pine are all good choices for this project.

Bittersweet Wreath

These berries are just as bright as holly, and cheaper, too.

Cut bright red bittersweet berries in small clusters from branches, and glue onto small (3- to 4-inch plastic-foam) wreath forms until base is no longer visible. Attach with bright satin ribbons to gift baskets, or hang about the house.

Fragrant Fire Starters

A pretty and fragrant way to start a fire!
They make good gifts, too.

MATERIALS:

6- to 8-inch long pieces of
  pine and balsa branches
dried heather and lavender
rosemary

thyme
3 long cinnamon sticks
raffia ribbon

Gather together the above ingredients and tie together with raffia ribbon, making a bow.

7

Crafts to Give Away

Lord, You gave us the best gift of all—Yourself.
As I make these simple gifts, may I give myself away as well.

Lacey Bottles

An inexpensive and lovely gift.

MATERIALS:

assorted bottles or small flower vases
lace motifs and trims as desired to fit bottles
   (available at craft and fabric stores)
Mod Podge (available from any craft store)
decoupage medium
small paintbrush

Experiment with placement of lace on the bottle until you are pleased with the arrangement. In order to fit the curvature of the bottle, trim some of the connecting threads so the points can be spread out. Spread Mod Podge on the bottle with a paintbrush in the basic shape of the trim. Place the lace over the brushed area and cover thoroughly with Mod Podge; let dry.

Family Tree

A thoughtful present to give a grandparent.

MATERIALS:

18-inch-long paper-covered wire—
    example, 36 pieces for 18 family members
boxwood leaves
1½-inch photo of each family member
glue
dried flowers
ribbon
6- x 6-inch piece of 1½ inch thick green Styrofoam
sheet moss

Begin by twisting together all of the pieces of covered wire about 2 inches from the bottom and continue upwards about 6 inches. Fan the bottom pieces out to form the "roots" of the tree. At the top of the twist, begin to divide the "branches" into groups of 4, fanning them out on both sides of the tree. Separate the strands of each group of 4 and fan out also. Trim ends of branches with scissors when finished to achieve realistic tree shape. Glue a two-inch ribbon loop to each photo. Then glue around perimeter of each photo and sprinkle with dried flowers to create frame effect. Cover Styrofoam with sheet moss and stick roots of tree in Styrofoam. Glue boxwood leaves to tree branches to simulate an evergreen tree and hang photos of family members to tree in generational order.

Victorian
Potpourri Handkerchiefs

A pretty and feminine gift.

MATERIALS:

antique linen handkerchief   narrow satin ribbon
   (or a small doily)   potpourri

Lay the handkerchief flat on the table, right side up. Put a cup of potpourri in the middle, bring sides up, and tie with a pretty ribbon. Insert a few stems of dried flowers into the center.

Treasure Box

A wonderful gift to share with your little girl!

shoe box   wrapping paper
glue   old costume jewelry

Glue flowered wrapping paper over shoe box, inside and out. Fill box full of costume jewelry you no longer wear and tie up with a pretty ribbon.

Gift of Money Frames

*Add some personalized thoughtfulness to
a money gift for those on your list who
are difficult to buy for.*

Fold and place the bill (or bills) of money in a small, elegant picture frame—two gifts in one!

Vacation Memory Box

A loving gift of shared memories!

MATERIALS:

old wooden or cardboard box with an attached lid
glue
vacation souvenirs: postcards, ticket stubs,
   small amounts of money (if foreign),
   street maps, photos, seashells

Leave box standing open and glue small items such as money, stamps, or seashells around the edges of the box and lid. Arrange items of your choice decoratively throughout interior of box.

Scented Sentiments Favor

*These make delightful party favors
to leave at each place setting,
or in a basket near the door to give to parting guests.*

MATERIALS:

3- x 5-inch blank card stock tags
bayberry-scented votive candle in a glass holder
red, green, or gold tissue paper
curling ribbon

Inscribe the following old rhyme on each tag:

On Christmas Eve may this Bayberry Candle
As it burns down to the Socket
Make you remember God's Blessings
Even when there's no money in your Pocket!

Wrap each candle in a 4- x 8-inch piece of tissue paper, twisting paper about 2 inches in at both ends. Tie with several pieces of curled ribbon at each end and attach the tag to one of the ribbons.

Surprise Rolls

Great for stocking stuffers or may be hung on the tree.

MATERIALS:

cardboard tubing from wrapping paper, paper towels,
  wax paper, aluminum foil, or toilet tissue
brightly colored crepe paper
long piece of ribbon for curling
assorted candies, treats, and snacks

Cut tubes into equal length sections, (about 3½ inches long). Place the cardboard tube on paper and roll up, pinching paper together at one end and tying with a piece of curling ribbon. Fill tube with treats, pinch other end, and tie with more curling ribbon. Open twisted ends, and decorate with glue and glitter or Christmas stickers.

Almond Bunches

*Hang these from your tree,
and then give them away to Christmas visitors.*

MATERIALS:

2 4-inch squares of net
   (green and red, or 2 other contrasting colors)
3 sugared almonds
$\frac{1}{4}$-inch wide gold ribbon, 18 inches long

With 2 net squares, 1 on top of the other, place almonds in center of net and bring up corners to make a bag. Fold the ribbon in half and make a single stitch about 4 inches from the fold. Hold the ribbon loop behind the almond bunch and tie loose ends at the front in a bow.

Caliente Wreath

For the person on your list who loves to add fire and spice to food!

Attach dried red chile peppers to an 18-inch wreath form with florist wire and give as a gift, along with a book filled with south-western recipes!

Gilded Fruit Basket

Makes a nice gift for a hostess.

MATERIALS:

figs, kiwis, lady apples
egg whites
3 sheets of 18-karat gold leaf
(available at craft stores)
Q-tips
3-inch-wide gold or white ribbon

small woven wicket basket
brown paper bags, shredded
walnuts and pistachios in
  the shell
cellophane wrap

Paint egg white on fruit with a pastry brush. With Q-tip, pick up a bit of the gold leaf and dab on fruit. It will dissolve into pretty random patterns. Use the shredded brown paper to fill basket and place fruit, walnuts, and pistachios inside. Gather cellophane wrap at top and tie with a large bow.

Jingle Bell
Napkin Rings

Use these as napkin rings for your holiday guests—
and then they can take them home and hang them from their tree.

String little jingle bells on a wire using an empty paper towel roll
as form. Add a little red bow to each.

8

Gift Wrap, Cards, Notes, and Tags

May each greeting I write this year, Lord, spread the Good News of Your birth.

Potato Print Christmas Cards

These cards will save you money—
and making them is a great activity to do with children.

MATERIALS:

thin cardboard in different colors   potato
poster paints   knife

Cut out 8- x 4-inch rectangles from festive colored cardboard and fold in half. Cut a potato in half and using a felt tip pen, draw around desired shape, (star, holly, bell, tree) onto potato. Carefully cut around shape with a small kitchen knife. Dip surface of potato into a saucer of diluted poster paint and press potato firmly down on scrap paper to test. If print is sketchy, carefully slice off tip to make flatter. Print your cards!

Family Photo Wraps

This wrapping paper is truly one of a kind!

MATERIALS:

family photographs
white mat board in size desired
clear tape

Arrange photograph on white mat board, overlapping as desired. Secure backs of photographs to mat board with small rings of tape. Photocopy arrangement at a copy center in black and white to make your wrapping paper. Size can be reduced to use wrapping for smaller gifts.

Double Duty Cards

A practical and pretty way to recycle.

Use decorative fronts of last year's Christmas cards as this year's
gift tags. (Make sure there is no writing on back side!)

Rainbow Wrap

Children will enjoy creating this wrapping paper, too.

MATERIALS:

tableau paper or tissue paper, up to 24 inches square
red, green, blue, and yellow food coloring
water
muffin tin

Using cups of a muffin tin, mix water and food coloring to produce desired shades. Leave 1 cup for water only. Fold paper into 2-inch-wide accordion folds one way, then accordion fold into squares or triangles. Dip paper corners into water first, then into 1 or more different dyes. Blot folded paper between several sheets of newspaper, pressing hard. Remove paper and open carefully. Let dry on newspaper.

Doily Note Cards

A lovely way to personalize a Christmas note.

MATERIALS:

scraps of paper: parchment, watercolor, craft, or scrapbook
decorative-edged scissors   craft glue
assorted doilies   paper punch and thin ribbon

Cut paper in desired card size and fold in half. Trim edges of card with decorative-edged scissors. Trim doily to fit front of note card; glue in place. To use for a package tag, punch small holes in card to thread through the ribbon.

Socks Galore

A fun wrapping for the teenage girl in your life.

Buy a pair of novelty socks to use as wrapping for a selection of small presents. Tie socks together with a big wire-edged bow.

Recipe Greeting Card

This recipe turns your Christmas card into a special gift.

Print your own family greeting in calligraphy on cream-toned textured stock and include following recipe for mulled cider:

Mulled Cider

In a large pot, combine:

1 gallon of fresh apple cider	8 allspice berries
¼ cup brown sugar	1 tsp rum flavoring
12 whole cloves	6 split cinnamon sticks

Steep over very low heat for 20 minutes. Ladle into mugs and garnish each serving with a cinnamon stick. Makes 6 cups.

Leaf Wrap

Here's another wrapping that the children will want to help you make!

This will have to be done in early fall with an assortment of fresh leaves. Place leaves on a stamp pad, layer plastic wrap over top and gently rub with finger to ink leaf. Place leaf upside down on wrapping paper and cover with scrap paper; rub to print leaf designs.

Wrapping Materials
(common and uncommon)

Be creative and come up with your own ideas.

wallpaper leftovers
brightly colored scarves
decorative boxes
newspaper
fabric
metallic paper

needlework bags
cloth napkins
colored cellophane
tissue paper
foil

Econo Tags

For those who believe strongly in recycling.

Add gold stars or glitter to tags cut out of an old manila file folder and use as name tags.

All Tied Up

Fun, fancy—and simple!

Attach small jingle bells to unusually patterned shoelaces and use to tie up small packages.

It's in the Bag

*Easy, inexpensive, and thoughtful,
this "wrapping" works for almost any gift.*

MATERIALS:

gold spray paint
brown paper lunch or grocery bag
gold tissue paper

gold silk wire ribbon,
   3 inches wide
3 long cinnamon sticks

Spray-paint bag in a random fashion. Surround gift in tissue paper and place in bag with tissue spilling from top of bag. Wrap ribbon around bag (enclosing cinnamon sticks) and tie a pretty bow.

Berry Boxed

*Another simple and cheap way to
add country elegance to any gift.*

Weave gingham or plaid ribbon through slats of a strawberry basket and line with colored tissue. Place homemade goodies or cookies inside and wrap in clear cellophane.